A Catholic I

Catholics in the Public Square

Revised 4th Edition

Most Reverend Thomas J. Olmsted

Bishop of the Diocese of Phoenix

Foreword by

Jose H. Gomez
Archbishop of Los Angeles

SAINT BENEDICT+PRESS

ISBN: 978-1-61890-854-4

Published in the United States by
Saint Benedict Press
PO Box 410487
Charlotte, NC 28241
www.SaintBenedictPress.com

Printed and bound in the United States of America

This printing of

Catholics in the Public Square

by Most Rev. Thomas J. Olmsted

made possible through

the generous support of the

KNIGHTS
OF COLUMBUS®

TABLE OF CONTENTS

FOREWORD

Catholic social teaching gives us a vision of the world as it could be and as it should be. The world as God created it to be.

The gospel of Jesus Christ is the most radical doctrine in the history of ideas. If the world believed what Jesus proclaimed—that God is our Father and we are all brothers and sisters created in His image with God-given dignity and a transcendent destiny—every society could be transformed overnight.

Of course, human sin and weakness always stand in the way of God's beautiful plan for creation. Every structure of social injustice starts in the hearts of individuals. Societies do not sin, people do. So for Catholics, social reform means more than raising consciousness, expanding opportunities, and building new programs. Those things are necessary. But true justice and lasting peace require the conversion of hearts and the renewal of minds.

The Catholic vision is spiritual not political. Catholics belong first of all the "city of God." But we have a duty to build up the "city of man," to correct injustices and seek a world that reflects God's desires for His children — what Jesus called the kingdom of God and the Apostles called the new heaven and new earth.

The Church articulates universal principles that are rooted in the laws of nature and that reflect the wisdom the universal Church has gained in more than two thousand years of serving people under many different nations, cultural realities, government systems, and economic orders.

The motive and measure in everything we do is our concern to promote the flourishing of the human person. Our principles drive us to work for justice and the common good, to protect the vulnerable and lift up the weak, to promote freedom and human dignity, and to prefer remedies that are personal, local, and small-scale.

In twenty-first century America, the Church confronts a highly secularized and ethnically diversified society shaped by the economic forces of globalization, a technocratic mentality, and a consumerist lifestyle. Our society is centered on the individual self — with an often exaggerated preoccupation for individuals' unlimited rights and their freedoms for self-definition and self-invention. Happiness and meaning in American life are defined increasingly according to individualistic concerns for material pleasure and comfort. And we see many signs that, as a people, we are becoming more withdrawn from our communities and from the duties of our common life. More and more we seem less able to have empathy for those we don't know.

Pope Francis speaks of the "globalization of indifference" to suffering and cruelty in the world. And he is on to something.

In America and abroad, the people of our globalized society seem to tolerate a growing list of injustices and indignities. To name just a few: widespread abortion; the "quiet" euthanasia of the old and sick; birth control policies targeting the poor and "unfit"; racial discrimination; a widening gap between poor and rich; pollution of the environment, especially in poor and minority communities; pornography and drug addiction; the death penalty and scandalous conditions in our prisons; the erosion of religious liberty; and a broken immigration system that breaks up families and leaves a permanent underclass living in the shadows of our prosperity.

The Church's social teaching "speaks" to all of these issues. The *Compendium of the Social Doctrine of the Church*, an essential resource, is nearly five hundred pages long. But in the face of so many daily injustices that cry out to heaven, we can feel tempted to compartmentalize our compassion, to draw up lines of division about who and what we will care about.

For decades now, we have accepted a basic "fault-line" in the Church's social witness—between self-described "pro-life" Catholics and those who consider themselves "peace and justice" Catholics. This is a false divide and one that is a scandal to Christ and the Church's faithful witness in society.

God does not see the world through the limitations of our political categories of "left" and "right," "liberal" and "conservative." He is our Father and He sees only His children. When one of God's children is suffering injustice, He calls the rest of us to love and compassion and to "make things right." Our concern for human dignity and life can never be partial or a half-measure. How can we justify defending the dignity of some and not others or protecting God's creation while neglecting some of His most vulnerable creatures?

In some Church circles today we are seeing a return to the vision of a "seamless garment" or "consistent ethic of life."

Advocates have noble intentions — they want to bring the Church's moral wisdom and passion for justice to bear on a broad range of urgent issues. They recognize that the Church's social witness must be founded on our common responsibility to defend the gift of human life at every stage and in every condition.

In practice, however, this line of thinking can lead to a kind of moral relativism that renders serious social issues as more or less equivalent. Setting priorities and frameworks for decision-making becomes an arbitrary, sometimes partisan exercise in political calculation.

A broad desire to promote the integral development of the human person leads to obvious and crucial agenda items: abortion, euthanasia, capital punishment, global poverty and the related issues of migrants and refugees, and climate change. Each of these realities of our world represents an affront to human dignity and threatens the sustainability of social order.

But the hard truth is that not all injustices in the world are "equal." Perhaps we can understand this better about issues in the past than we can with issues in the present. For instance, we would never want to describe slavery as just one of several problems in eighteenth and nineteenth-century American life. There are indeed "lesser" evils. But that means there are also "greater" evils—evils that are more serious than others and even some evils that are so grave that Christians are called to address them as a primary duty.

Among the evils and injustices in American life in 2016, abortion and euthanasia are different and stand apart. Each is a direct, personal attack on innocent and vulnerable human life. Abortion and euthanasia function in our society as what the *Catechism of the Catholic Church* calls "structures of sin" or "social sins."

Both practices are sanctioned by the law of the land and supported, promoted, and even paid for as part of government policy. Abortion has become a part of mainstream health care and one of the "freedoms" that Americans presume. Euthanasia or doctor-assisted suicide is fast gaining that same status. Both practices are zealously defended by our society's elites—those who shape public opinion and civic morality through government, the popular media, and education.

Our society's elites tell us that abortion and euthanasia are private, deeply personal matters that ultimately should concern only the individuals involved. If that were really true, these issues would not be matters for public policy and subjects of constant advocacy and litigation.

Evils and injustices committed behind closed doors are still evil and unjust and are never only personal but have consequences and implications for our life together. And the Church is called to speak the truth and to confront the idols of the human heart and the idols of society. As Pope Francis has said: "It is not licit to eliminate a human life to solve a problem. . . . [It is] a sin against God the Creator: think hard about this."

This is the great challenge for the Church's social witness in our society, which seeks to address many of its problems through the elimination of human life—not only through abortion and assisted suicide, but also in the areas of the death penalty, human embryo research, and mandated contraception.

It is this broader mentality—what Francis and previous popes have called a "culture of death"—that the Church must confront. That is why abortion and euthanasia are not just two issues among many or only questions of individual conscience. Abortion and euthanasia raise basic questions of human rights and social justice, questions of what kind of society and what kind of people we want to be. Do we really want to become a people that responds to human suffering by helping to kill the one who suffers? Do we really want to be a society where the lives of the weak are sacrificed for the comfort and benefit of those who are stronger? That is why any approach that essentially tolerates abortion and euthanasia or puts these issues on par with others, not only betrays the beautiful vision of the Church's social teaching, but also weakens the credibility of the Church's witness in our society.

The Church must continue to insist that the fundamental injustice and violence in our society is the direct killing of those who are not yet born through abortion and those who are sick and at the end of their lives through euthanasia and assisted suicide. In this culture, the Church must insist that abortion and euthanasia are grave and intrinsic evils—evils that are corrosive and corrupting, evils that are at the heart of other social injustices.

Abortion and euthanasia are "fundamental" social issues because if the child in the womb has no right to be born, if the sick and the old have no right to be taken care of, then there is no solid foundation to defend anyone's human rights, and no foundation for peace and justice in society. How can we claim to speak for the marginalized and disenfranchised, if we are allowing millions of innocent children to be killed each year in the womb? If we cannot justify caring for the weakest and most innocent of God's creatures, how can we call our society to resist the excesses of nationalism and militarism or confront global poverty or protect our common home in creation?

In broader terms, the Church faces an unprecedented challenge in the America that is emerging in the twenty-first century. This is perhaps the most disturbing sign for our nation's future: the increasing hostility and discrimination against Christian institutions and the vilifying of Christian beliefs by the government, the courts, the media, and popular culture. More and more in our country we see religious faith marginalized as something that is "personal" and "private." Catholics and other believers face strong pressures to keep their faith to themselves and to live as if their beliefs should not have any influence on how they live in society or carry out their duties as citizens.

The Church's social witness today—all our works of mercy and charity, all our advocacy for moral principles and human rights—now operates in an atmosphere of widespread confusion about the meaning of human life and the purpose of social institutions at every level.

To evangelize in this culture, the Church must articulate a new Christian humanism, a new vision of human flourishing that is rooted in God's beautiful plan of love for creation and for every human life. Our new evangelization must be a new proclamation of the Kingdom—as a city of love and truth where every life is welcomed, cherished, and defended, especially those lives that need more care and attention, those lives that can be a burden to others. Our new evangelization must seek a society worthy of the sanctity and dignity of the human person, where no one is a stranger and no one is left behind or thrown away.

Our humanism must be more than words. It must be expressed in actions, in works of mercy. Wherever dignity is denied and wherever there is injustice, we are called to defend life. Our society must know that, as long as there are Christians, there should never be a reason for anyone to suffer without hope and help.

The Church needs clear and courageous teaching and witness to confront the idols of a secularized, post-Christian America. For many years now, my friend Bishop Thomas Olmsted of Phoenix has been one of the Church's clearest and most courageous teachers and leaders. In his ministry we see all the essentials of the new Christian humanism that is called for in our times.

I welcome this fourth edition of Bishop Olmsted's widely read and influential *Catholics in the Public Square*. This book is a kind of "question and answer catechism" on some of the deepest issues of faith and public life. Bishop Olmsted is a wise and prudent guide, and over the years, I find I am still learning from him.

As he writes in this new edition: "It is our duty to engage the culture, not run from it. We must place our trust in the Lord and know that by doing His will and speaking the truth in love, God will make all things work for the good. It is also the duty of the Catholic faithful to support courageous people who do this through both our actions and prayers."

Catholics in the Public Square is a must-read for all of us who are trying to engage the culture and to proclaim the Church's beautiful vision for human life and human society. I pray that this book will be widely read and widely lived.

✠ *Most Reverend José H. Gomez*
   Archbishop of Los Angeles
   March 2016

1) How would you define a lay person?

> A lay person is any member of the faithful who has not received Holy Orders and does not belong to a religious state approved by the Church. Through Baptism, a lay person is incorporated into Christ and becomes integrated into the People of God. A lay person has an important role in the life and mission of the Church. (*Lumen Gentium*, 31)

When Pope John Paul II wrote his major work on the life and mission of the laity he titled it *Christifideles Laici*, Christ's faithful laity. With this title he made it clear that faithful love of Christ is the key to bearing fruit in the kingdom of God. This is true for everyone in the Church, not only the laity. Jesus says, "I am the vine, you are the branches. Whoever remains in me and I in him will bear much fruit, because without me you can do nothing" (Jn 15:5).

2) What is the difference between the laity and the clergy in the Catholic Church?

The clergy receive a special charism of the Holy Spirit through the Sacrament of Holy Orders. As such, deacons, priests, and bishops "realize a participation in the priesthood of Jesus Christ that is different, not simply in degree but in essence, from the participation given to the lay faithful through Baptism and Confirmation" (*Christifideles Laici*, 22).

Laypersons, meanwhile, are primarily concerned with temporal matters and as such have a sort of "secular character." The laity may also be involved in matters connected with pastoral ministry but only in matters that do not require the grace of Holy Orders.

3) What is the role of the laity in the Catholic Church?

The role of the laity is in a special way to "seek the kingdom of God by engaging in temporal affairs and ordering them according to the plan of God" (*Lumen Gentium*, 31). As such, lay men and women are in a unique position to bring their faith into all areas of society.

It should be remembered that as the laity engage in temporal affairs, in their own way, they participate in the priestly, prophetic, and kingly mission of the Church by virtue of their Baptism and Confirmation.

4) How do Catholic laypersons fulfill their call to holiness?

Every Catholic receives from God a call to holiness that is rooted in Baptism. In order to fulfill this call, lay men and women are required to "follow and imitate Jesus Christ in embracing the Beatitudes; in listening and meditating on the Word of God; in conscious and active participation in the liturgical and sacramental life of the Church; in personal prayer; in family or in community; in the hunger and thirst for justice; in the practice of the commandment of love in all circumstances of life and service to the brethren, especially in the least, the poor and the suffering" (*Christifideles Laici*, 16).

5) What are the main responsibilities of Catholics to themselves?

Catholics have the responsibility of accepting Christ's invitation, "Come, follow me." They need to surrender in love as He leads them along the paths of conversion, communion, and solidarity (cf. *Ecclesia in America*). They also need to properly form themselves in the Church's teaching, participate actively in her sacramental life, and live their faith in God accordingly. This responsibility exists for Catholics in all states of life.

Accordingly, Catholics are to be "ever mindful of what it means to be members of the Church of Jesus Christ, participants in her mystery of communion and in her dynamism in mission and the apostolate" (*Christifideles Laici*, 64).

6) What are the main responsibilities of Catholics to their families?

Marriage is the foundation of the family. The family, in turn, is the basic cell of society. Marriage and family responsibilities are, therefore, of tremendous importance, not only to the Church, but also to all of society.

The responsibilities of Catholic men and women to their families cannot be overstated. "It is above all the lay faithful's duty in the apostolate to make the family aware of its identity as the primary social nucleus, and its basic role in society, so that it might itself become always a more active and responsible place for proper growth and proper participation in social life" (*Christifideles Laici*, 40).

7) What are the responsibilities of the Catholic laity in the public square?

Through their baptism, the laity is called to holiness of life (i.e. to live their faith in God day in and day out). Their responsibilities are not meant to be merely a matter of personal piety or devotion, but also directed toward evangelization in all aspects of life.

A lay person in the public square has a particular responsibility to live his or her vocation in view of its unique impact on society. For example, those involved with the noble art of politics, or the legal profession, often are in a position to influence societal norms on matters of real significance by working on legislative proposals or judicial proceedings aimed at preserving the inalienable rights of all persons, rights that are grounded in the natural law upon which our country was founded.

Similarly, there are others in the public square that while not serving as elected officials or officers of the court, nonetheless, are in a position to shape the society and culture. For these individuals, especially those involved with all forms of the mass media, a significant part of their responsibilities is to live their faith by promoting the common good in society.

8) How do Catholics show their own identity in public life?

Catholics should always be respectful of the human dignity of others, including people of different faiths, or no faith at all. Having said that, however, Catholics should not be afraid to embrace their identity or to put their faith into practice in public life. In fact, each of the faithful has a call to evangelization and to share the good news of Christ with the rest of the world.

9) What difference should Catholics make in public life?

There are multitudes of different ways in which Catholics may serve the Church through their contributions in public life. In each circumstance, however, Catholics are especially called to contribute to the common good, to defend the dignity of every human person, and to live as faithful citizens.

In this sense, the final result that takes place is ultimately in God's hands. This fact is important to remember when a Catholic is in a distinctly minority position and unable to accomplish a desired result. It is in these seemingly hopeless circumstances that Catholics who provide a faithful witness in public life can often be used by God to touch hearts and minds in ways that may not always be visible to the naked eye.

It is good to remember Pope Benedict's words: "There are times when the burden of need and our own limitations might tempt us to become discouraged. But precisely then we are helped by the knowledge that, in the end, we are only instruments in the Lord's hands; and this knowledge frees us from the presumption of thinking that we alone are personally responsible for building a better world. In all humility we will do what we can, and in all humility we will entrust the rest to the Lord" (*Deus Caritas Est*, 35).

10) How should Catholics understand the separation between Church and state?

The separation of Church and state all too often is used as an excuse to silence people of faith and to discourage them from legitimately participating in the public square. The First Amendment of the United States Constitution, of course, does not advocate for a separation of Church and state at all, but rather the protection of religious freedom from the state.

Our founding fathers intended all persons to have the equal right to voice their opinions, including those based on religious convictions. Even more, they understood that it was imperative that the state not infringe upon the religious beliefs of its citizens. The Constitution is aimed at allowing all people to have a voice in government, including those whose voice is distinctively religious.

In other words, there is nothing in the Constitution excluding people from bringing their faith into the public square.

As Pope Francis said in an address in Philadelphia on September 26, 2015, "Religious freedom certainly means the right to worship God, individually and in community, as our consciences dictate. But religious liberty, by its nature, transcends places of worship and the private sphere of individuals and families."

11) Should Catholics bring the Church's doctrine into the public square?

There are times when the Church's intervention in social questions is needed. As the *Compendium of the Catechism of the Catholic Church* teaches, "the Church intervenes by making a moral judgment about economic and social matters when the fundamental rights of the person, the common good, or the salvation of souls requires it" (510).

When Pope Benedict XVI visited the United States in April 2008, he told the American Bishops, "Any tendency to treat religion as a private matter must be resisted. Only when their faith permeates every aspect of their lives do Christians become truly open to the transforming power of the Gospel."

Pope Francis continued on this theme during his visit to the United States in September 2015 when he said, "In a world where various forms of modern tyranny seek to suppress religious freedom, or try to reduce it to a subculture without right to a voice in the public square, or to use religion as a pretext for hatred and brutality, it is imperative that the followers of the various religions join their voices in calling for peace, tolerance, and respect for the dignity of others."

While Catholics are called to bring their faith and religious views into the public square, they are also called to respect the religious freedom and civil liberties of all people. In fact, the Church has genuine respect for secular governments that afford these protections to people of all faiths, as well as those without faith.

In reality, the Church does not impose its doctrine on others in the public square. For example, there is no effort by the Church to compel the public to attend Mass on Sundays or receive various sacraments. Nonetheless, the Church is legitimately concerned about many matters of societal importance and brings its views to bear in proposing meaningful solutions for promoting the common good.

12) How do you respond to statements that Catholics should not impose their religious views upon others?

Some Catholics and other believers have been frightened into silence and even confused by charges that they are imposing their morality on others. It is contended that a person's faith should have no impact on his or her public life. This leads to the infamous "I am a Catholic but . . ." syndrome! Of course, if one's faith does not impact on one's whole life, including one's political and social responsibilities, then it is not authentic faith; it is a sham, a counterfeit.

A democratic society needs the active participation of all its citizens, people of faith included. People of faith engage issues on the basis of what they believe, just as atheists engage issues on the basis of what they hold dear; they fight for what they think is right and oppose what they consider wrong. This is not an imposition on other's morality. It is acting with integrity. Moreover, people of genuine faith strengthen the whole moral fabric of a country. The active engagement of Catholics in democratic processes is good for society and it is responsible citizenship.

13) Should Catholics take into account their own faith at the moment of voting?

It only makes sense that if Catholics are supposed to live their faith in all of their daily activities that they should also take their faith into account while voting. As noted in the Second Vatican Council's teaching, "every citizen ought to be mindful of his right and his duty to promote the common good by using his vote" (*Gaudium et Spes*, 75).

In preparing to vote, Catholics need to understand their faith so that their consciences are properly formed. Subsequent to this formation, it is important to research all of the important issues and candidates that will appear on the ballot. Only after sufficient preparation and prayer, is a Catholic fully ready to discharge his or her responsibilities as a faithful citizen and cast a meaningful vote.

14) Can Catholics honestly disagree in matters of politics, social, or cultural issues?

In 2002, the Congregation for the Doctrine of the Faith issued a document entitled *Doctrinal Note on Some Questions Regarding Participation of Catholics in Political Life* that addresses the existence of political matters in which Catholics may disagree. There are, indeed, many issues upon which Catholics may legitimately differ such as the best methods to achieve welfare reform or to address illegal immigration.

Conversely, however, there are other issues that are intrinsically evil[1] and can never legitimately be supported. For example, Catholics may never legitimately promote or vote for any law that attacks innocent human life.

---

[1] Traditionally, the Church has referred to such moral acts as "intrinsically evil." Such acts can never result in good, no matter the circumstances.

15) What does it mean that Catholics should follow their conscience when making a moral decision?

Before following our conscience, we must form it in accord with the voice of God. Our conscience is not the origin of truth. Truth lies outside us; it exists independent of us and must be discovered through constant effort of mind and heart. This is no easy task for us who suffer the effects of original sin and must contend with the constant temptations of the devil. Conscience receives the truth revealed by God and discerns how to apply that truth to concrete circumstances.

The *Catechism of the Catholic Church* teaches, "Conscience must be informed and moral judgment enlightened. A well-informed conscience is upright and truthful. It formulates its judgments according to reason, in conformity with the true good willed by the wisdom of the Creator. The education of conscience is indispensable for human beings who are subjected to negative influences and tempted by sin to prefer their own judgment and to reject authoritative teachings" (1783).

As we see, to form one's own conscience well and to follow it with integrity is no small task. For a person's conscience cannot invent what is true and good. It must search it out beyond itself. When acting correctly, we discover the truth through the grace of the Holy Spirit and the help of God's word handed down to us in the Church. Then, when we submit our conscience to this objective truth, we act uprightly and grow to maturity in Christ.

16) Is it mandatory for Catholics to follow what the Pope or bishops say on political issues?

Because they are the leaders of the Church, it is always important to respect statements from the Church's hierarchy. It is the role of the Pope and the bishops to teach clearly on matters of faith and morals, including those touching on political issues.

There are some matters, however, on which Catholics may disagree with the Church's hierarchy. In some cases, for example, a Catholic may agree with the teaching of the Church, but come to a different prudential judgment about its application.

Examples of these issues might include an instance where someone agrees with the Church's teaching on "just war" or "capital punishment," but reaches a different conclusion as to whether the facts of the situation constitute a "just war" or the "rare" circumstances where capital punishment may be used under Church teaching.

It should be emphasized, however, that despite these examples, there are other issues, such as abortion or euthanasia, that are always wrong and do not allow for the correct use of prudential judgment to justify them. It would never be proper for Catholics to be on the opposite side of these issues.

17) Are all political and social issues equal when it comes to choosing a political candidate?

Absolutely not! The Catholic Church is actively engaged in a wide variety of important public policy issues including immigration, education, affordable housing, health, and welfare, to name just a few. On each of these issues we should do our best to be informed and to support those proposed solutions that seem most likely to be effective. However, when it comes to direct attacks on innocent human life, being right on all the other issues can never justify a wrong choice on this most serious matter.

As Pope John Paul II has written, "Above all, the common outcry, which is justly made on behalf of human rights—for example, the right to health, to home, to work, to family, to culture—is false and illusory if the right to life, the most basic and fundamental right and the condition for all other personal rights, is not defended with the maximum determination" (*Christifideles Laici*, 38).

18) Are there any "non-negotiable" issues for Catholics involved in politics?

There are several issues that are "not negotiable" for Catholics in political life, because they involve matters that are always wrong given their nature. In an address to European politicians on March 30, 2006, Pope Benedict XVI stated: "As far as the Catholic Church is concerned, the principal focus of her interventions in the public arena is the protection and promotion of the dignity of the person, and she is thereby consciously drawing particular attention to principles which are not negotiable. Among these the following emerge clearly today:

- Protection of life in all its stages, from the first moment of conception until natural death;

- Recognition and promotion of the natural structure of the family—as a union between a man and a woman based on marriage—and its defense from attempts to make it juridically equivalent to radically different forms of union which in reality harm it and contribute to its destabilization, obscuring its particular character and its irreplaceable social role;

- The protection of the rights of parents to educate their children."

The issues mentioned by Pope Benedict are all "non-negotiable" and are some of the most contemporary issues in the political arena. I should note, however, that other issues, while not necessarily "non-negotiable," are tremendously important and deserve prayerful consideration, such as questions of war and capital punishment, poverty issues, how to best care for our environment, and matters relating to illegal immigration.

19) What are the causes that can ban Catholics from Holy Communion?

No one who is conscious of having committed a serious sin should receive Holy Communion. For the Eucharist is the very Body and Blood of Jesus Christ, our most precious gift in the Church. And St. Paul warns us: "Whoever eats the bread or drinks the cup of the Lord unworthily will have to answer for the body and blood of the Lord. A person should examine himself, and so eat the bread and drink the cup. For anyone who eats and drinks without discerning the body, eats and drinks judgment on himself" (I Cor 11:27–29).

All Catholics should examine their consciences, and refrain from receiving Holy Communion if they are not living in a proper state of grace. Should some Catholic politicians who are presently pro-abortion obstinately persist in this contradiction to our faith, this becomes a source of scandal. In these and similar cases, measures beyond those of moral persuasion may need to be taken by those in leadership in the Church. As God tells us in the Book of Leviticus, "You shall not stand by idly when your neighbor's life is at stake" (19:16).

If a politician is actively supporting and furthering the culture of death, he is not only causing scandal; he is sinning. Similarly, when a politician performs actions (like voting) that allow for abortions and even promote abortions, or that mandate the distribution of contraceptives by pharmacists and others, that politician is materially cooperating in grave sin. When this occurs, then the politician cannot receive Holy Communion without previously making a good confession. A good confession would require sincere sorrow for such sin and a firm purpose of making amendment. Since the harm done would be public in nature, the amendment should also be public.

20) Why does the Church set such high standards for Catholics?

The high standards to which Catholics (and all Christians) are called come from Christ. We find them in the Sacred Scriptures. For example, Jesus said, "If you love me, you will keep my commandments" (Jn 14:15). He also said, "Whoever wishes to come after me must deny himself, take up his cross, and follow me. For whoever wishes to save his life will lose it, but whoever loses his life for my sake and that of the Gospel will save it. What profit is there for one to gain the whole world and forfeit his life?" (Mk 8:34–36).

We also find in the Sacred Scriptures admonitions such as those of St. Paul to Timothy where he writes, "Proclaim the word; be persistent whether it is convenient or inconvenient; convince, reprimand, encourage through all patience and teaching. For the time will come when people will not tolerate sound doctrine but, following their own desires and insatiable curiosity, will accumulate teachers and will stop listening to the truth and will be diverted to myths. But you, be self-possessed in all circumstances; put up with hardship; perform the work of an evangelist; fulfill your ministry" (I Tim 4:2–5).

There are cases where Catholics in public life serve with great courage and distinction. They measure up to the high standards set by Christ. There are others, sadly, who obstinately persist in manifest grave sin where the risk of scandal is great. In the matter of abortion, for example, abortion is the killing of a completely innocent life and thus bad news for both unborn children and their mothers. It is a horrible wrong. It is intrinsically evil.

We have a serious obligation to protect human life, and especially the lives of the most innocent and vulnerable among us. Whoever fails to do this, when otherwise able to do so, commits serious sins of omission. They jeopardize their own spiritual wellbeing and they are a source of scandal for others. Should they be Catholics, they should not receive Holy Communion.

21) Can Catholics belong to or express support for different political parties?

The Church is never partisan and does not endorse political candidates. She does, however, encourage her laity to be involved in political parties in order to devote themselves to promoting the common good. In this regard, political and civic education is deemed necessary so that all citizens will be able to play a part in political affairs. (See *Gaudium et Spes*, 75.)

22) Do bishops and priests have the right to intervene in political, social, or cultural matters?

Bishops and priests are not to participate in the public administration of the government. Nonetheless, they do have the right, and sometimes an obligation, to speak out on political, social, or cultural matters impacting the Church or the common good.

In his encyclical *Deus Caritas Est*, Pope Benedict XVI states: "It is not the Church's responsibility to make this teaching prevail in political life. Rather, the Church wishes to help form consciences in political life and to stimulate greater insight into the authentic requirements of justice as well as greater readiness to act accordingly, even when this might involve conflict with situations of personal interest" (28).

The Holy Father goes on to write: "The Church cannot and must not take upon herself the political battle to bring about the most just society possible. She cannot and must not replace the State. Yet at the same time she cannot and must not remain on the sidelines in the fight for justice. She has to play her part through rational argument and she has to awaken the spiritual energy without which justice, which always demands sacrifice, cannot prevail and prosper" (*ibid.*).

23) If bishops and priests can intervene in public issues, what is the difference then between the clergy and the laity in public policy issues?

While bishops and priests can appropriately speak out on important issues, the laity can be involved to a much larger degree. Unlike members of the clergy, the laity, in fact, are called to play a role in all areas of political involvement, including partisan politics and the administration of government.

Members of the laity generally have no restrictions in holding elective office or running the affairs of the state, while members of the clergy are generally prohibited from holding such positions.

24) What can Catholics do to foster justice in society?

There is much that Catholics can do to foster justice in society. A significant part of fostering justice is concern for the human dignity of all people—especially the poor, marginalized, or vulnerable. A concern for justice must always be mindful of Christ's forgiveness and mercy.

Pope Francis reminded us of this fact during his address to the United Nations General Assembly in September 2015, when he said, "The common home of all men and women must continue to rise on the foundations of a right understanding of universal fraternity and respect for the sacredness of every man and every woman, the poor, the elderly, children, the infirm, the unborn, the unemployed, the abandoned, those considered disposable because they are only considered part of a statistic."

Thankfully, the promotion of justice can be found in many Church agencies, including those serving the homeless, immigrants, prisoners, disabled people, and the elderly to name just a few. Catholics must always have a concern for justice and are encouraged to promote it not only in the public square, but also in volunteer efforts as well as their everyday lives.

25) What are the responsibilities of Catholics who own or operate businesses toward their employees and the society at large?

By virtue of their position, Catholics who are responsible for businesses have unique responsibilities to both their employees and the society at large. Catholic Social Teaching supports them in their private businesses while reminding them of their duty to respect the human dignity of their employees.

In fact, all businesses have a duty to respect the human dignity of their employees and to treat them fairly. While it is true that a primary reason that businesses exist is for the creation of profit, nonetheless it would be wrong for them to focus exclusively or excessively on the maximization of profit without regard for the welfare of employees and the communities they serve.

It is worth noting that influential Catholics in the business world, like all others, have an obligation to share of their time, talent, and treasure. People of extraordinary means are in a unique position to greatly assist both the Church and society through their participation in various philanthropic, charitable, educational, and even political efforts that respect life and promote the common good.

26) How can Catholics contribute to a culture of life?

Catholics can contribute to a "culture of life" in much the same way that they can promote justice, peace, and human dignity. There are a plethora of volunteer opportunities to assist in crisis pregnancy centers, hospices, nursing homes, and many other facilities.

Additionally, Catholics are called to advocate and to work for a "culture of life" by making it an issue of constant importance in political debate and in the public square.

Finally, prayer is a primary means of promoting and fostering a "culture of life." While personal daily prayer is always important, public prayer gatherings can provide a striking witness to the rest of society.

27) What means should Catholics employ to manifest their convictions about issues in the public square?

There are various means that Catholics may legitimately employ to manifest their convictions about issues in the public square. Catholic elected officials, for example, are in a privileged position to make known their opposition to public policy issues that are intrinsically evil.

Because of the democracy in which we live, even those who are not in political life have an opportunity and responsibility to express their opinions on various issues and to vote in elections.

Although voting is an important way of expressing convictions about issues, Catholics need not wait for elections to express their views. Letters to the editor, organized public events, and communicating with elected officials are also good examples of expressing views and bringing about change in the public square.

28) Should Catholics put aside their faith to work with people of other religions in social issues?

Catholics are called to live their faith in all that they do, including dialogue and collaboration with ecumenical or interreligious organizations. Activities such as prayer, dialogue, and various community service projects with people of other beliefs are all commendable, especially when the participants are well formed in their faith. Such action, if authentic, would never necessitate setting aside one's faith in order to participate.

29) What are the responsibilities of Catholic institutions in the public square?

There are a wide variety of Catholic institutions performing great works around the world, including numerous charitable organizations, hospitals, schools, and universities. In our own country, we have long been blessed by the high quality and caring service that these institutions provide, especially to the most vulnerable in our society.

Part of the reason these institutions are so remarkable is because of their fidelity to the Church and their desire stemming from the Catholic faith to promote the common good. When Catholic institutions are faithful to their identity and mission, they are fulfilling their responsibilities in the public square, and God works wondrous deeds through them.

Unfortunately, many Catholic institutions are currently under pressure to abandon their identity and mission, and to become just like any other secular organization. Catholic institutions, however, have a serious responsibility to resist such temptations, mindful that no good can be accomplished without God.

As our Holy Father has stated in his book *Jesus of Nazareth*: "[w]hen God is regarded as a secondary matter that can be set aside temporarily or permanently on account of more important things, it is precisely these supposedly more important things that come to nothing" (p. 33).

While Catholic institutions can be a great witness to our faith by virtue of their work in the public square, they can also be a source of scandal. In this regard, it is important that these institutions serve the common good and refrain from all words and actions that are contrary to the faith.

To this end, the Church rightly objects to recent government attempts to compel participation by Catholic institutions in abortions, homosexual adoptions, and any other matter that would compromise their responsibility to fulfill their identity and mission.

30) How does one best fight against secularization in our society and the misrepresentation of faith in the public square?

Unfortunately, discrimination against people of faith, and especially Catholics, is a real problem. A faithful Catholic in public life is almost certain to encounter forms of unjust discrimination and prejudice. There are many examples of unfavorable public misrepresentation of the Catholic faith and even outright hostility to people of any faith. While much progress has been made in protecting civil rights in our country, there remains a strong bias against people of faith in significant sectors of the media and certain segments of our society.

Nonetheless, it is our duty to engage the culture, not run from it. We must place our trust in the Lord and know that by doing His will and speaking the truth in love, God will make all things work for the good. It is also the duty of the Catholic faithful to support courageous people who do this through both our actions and prayers.

31) How would you define a "candidate who is a faithful Catholic?"

There are a large number of candidates or politicians in our country that label themselves as Catholic. Regrettably, however, some of these are an embarrassment to the Church and a scandal to others by virtue of their support of issues that, given their nature, can never be morally justified.

A candidate who is authentically Catholic is one who always defends the dignity of every human person and who puts the welfare of the common good over various partisan or self interests. His personal and public life is shaped by faith in Christ and His teachings. Such a candidate can be from any political party, but will never support matters that are "non-negotiable" such as abortion, euthanasia, embryonic stem cell research, human cloning, or "same-sex marriage."

32) What is the Church's position on immigration

The immigration issues facing our country today are extraordinarily complex and do not lend themselves to easy answers and simple solutions. Nonetheless, there are certain principles of Catholic Teaching that are relevant in addressing these matters.

The Church clearly recognizes the right of the state to control its borders. At the same time, as Pope John Paul II stated, "the Church in America must be a vigilant advocate, defending against any unjust restriction of the natural right of individual persons to move freely within their own nation and from one nation to another. Attention must be called to the rights of migrants and their families and to respect for their human dignity, even in cases of non-legal immigration" (*Ecclesia in America*, 65).

As our country works to address these complex issues, progress will only be possible when pursued through candid and courteous dialogue and respect for the human dignity of all. We do well to remember Pope Benedict's words to the U.S. Bishops (April 16, 2008), "I want to encourage you and your communities to continue to welcome the immigrants who join your ranks today, to share their joys and hopes, to support them in their sorrows and trials, and to help them flourish in their new home. This, indeed, is what your fellow countrymen have done for generations. From the beginning, they have opened their doors to the tired, the poor, the 'huddled masses yearning to breathe free' (cf. Sonnet inscribed on the Statue of Liberty). These are the people whom America has made her own."

In a September 2015 address to immigrants in Philadelphia, Pope Francis also noted that immigrants have responsibilities when he remarked, "You are called to be responsible citizens and to contribute as did those who came before, with so much effort; to contribute fruitfully to the life of the communities in which you live. I think in particular of the vibrant faith which so many of you possess, the deep sense of family life and all these other values which you have inherited. By contributing your gifts, you will not only find your place here, you will help to renew society from within."

33) What line should an elected official draw between his faith and his political commitments?

Elected officials should bring their faith to bear on all of their activities, including public affairs. In living out their faith, they should have a proper respect for the civil liberties of all people, including those of other faiths, or with no faith at all.

It should be pointed out, however, that sometimes Catholic politicians mistakenly claim that they need to abandon their faith out of an obligation to respect those of differing opinions or to honor a political commitment inherent with their office. These claims are perhaps most frequently made when Catholic politicians claim to be personally opposed to the killing of innocent unborn children.

Incredibly, it is somehow claimed by such people that it would be inappropriate to support legislation protecting human life because doing so would impose their faith on others or somehow violate their oath of office. These claims are ludicrous. Protecting human life is not only a religious imperative, it is a human imperative, and it is an imperative for all people.

People of faith have every right to bring their beliefs into the public square just like anyone else. In fact, Catholic elected officials should always live out their faith while promoting the welfare of all, including the protection of innocent human life.

34) How serious are the current threats to religious freedom in the United States?

The United States was founded on the principle of religious freedom and therefore it is of pivotal importance for all Americans. Religious liberty is particularly important for Catholics who are called, especially at this time in history, to unite with those of other faiths and people of good will to protect this fundamental freedom.

There are a number of extremely serious threats to religious freedom happening now in the United States and around the world. In our country, one of these threats has come in the form of government efforts to coerce those with religious objections to pay for or to provide health care coverage that includes intrinsic evils such as abortifacients and contraceptives. Another severe threat includes government coercion against those who do not want to participate in so-called "same-sex wedding ceremonies" because of deeply held religious beliefs that marriage, by its very nature, exclusively involves one man and one woman.

Pope Benedict addressed these concerns in an address to U.S. bishops on January 19, 2012 in which he stated: "In light of these considerations, it is imperative that the entire Catholic community in the United States come to realize the grave threats to the Church's public moral witness presented by a radical secularism which finds increasing expression in the political and cultural spheres. The seriousness of these threats needs to be clearly appreciated at every level of ecclesial life. Of particular concern are certain attempts being made to limit that most cherished of American freedoms, the freedom of religion."

The Holy Father went on in this address to observe what can be considered "a worrying tendency to reduce religious freedom to mere freedom of worship without guarantees of respect for freedom of conscience."

Regrettably, these threats continue to remain very real. As Pope Francis noted in an address at the White House on September 23, 2015, "With countless other people of good will, American Catholics are likewise concerned that efforts to build a just and wisely ordered society respect their deepest concerns and their right to religious liberty. That freedom remains one of America's most precious possessions. And, as my brothers, the United States bishops, have reminded us, all are called to be vigilant, precisely as good citizens, to preserve and defend that freedom from everything that would threaten or compromise it."

35) Do Catholic employers violate the religious freedom of their non-Catholic employees when they do not provide abortifacients or contraceptives in their health plans?

Even if there were a religion whose faith somehow contended that others needed to pay for their members' contraceptives or abortifacients, this frequently made claim reflects a serious misunderstanding of religious freedom; and it makes no sense on its face. The fact that an employer objects in conscience to paying for these items in no way violates anyone else's religious freedom.

The Catholic Church does not impose its faith on others; in fact, she believes that doing so is a serious violation of human dignity. But we are not dealing here with any imposition of our faith. We are merely defending our God-given freedom. It is deeply troubling that a significant number in our society today are trying to force others to violate their deeply held faith convictions, especially as it pertains to marriage and the family.

Thankfully, there are many people of various faiths who strongly share our conviction about religious freedom and are standing with us for this first and fundamental civil liberty. After all, disregard for religious freedom is not only a serious concern for the Catholic Church, but is simply un-American.

36) How can Catholics live in a manner that shows proper respect for God's creation?

We are called to be good stewards and respect all of God's creation. This responsibility extends first to each other as human beings created in God's own image, but also includes other living things, and all of creation.

As Pope Francis has written, "Care for nature is part of a lifestyle which includes the capacity for living together and communion. Jesus reminded us that we have God as our common Father and that this makes us brothers and sisters. Fraternal love can only be gratuitous; it can never be a means of repaying others for what they have done or will do for us. That is why it is possible to love our enemies. This same gratuitousness inspires us to love and accept the wind, the sun and the clouds, even though we cannot control them. In this sense, we can speak of a "universal fraternity" (*Laudato Si'*, 228).

In this regard, the Holy Father goes on to say, "It is enough to recognize that our body itself establishes us in a direct relationship with the environment and with other living beings. The acceptance of our bodies as God's gift is vital for welcoming and accepting the entire world as a gift from the Father and our common home, whereas thinking that we enjoy absolute power over our own bodies turns, often subtly, into thinking that we enjoy absolute power over creation" (*Laudato Si'*, 155).

Catholics in the Public Square: A Study in Conflict and Influence

Taught by Bradley Birzer, Ph.D.

Although John F. Kennedy proclaimed an "absolute" separation of church and state, faithful Catholics have long struggled to maintain a connection between faith and politics.

The intersection between church and state has always been a sticking point for Americans, especially for those in public office. During recent election cycles, we've witnessed spiritual compromise by self-described Catholic politicians and the attack of popular media against socially conservative candidates. Although Americans might not enjoy the same unity of Christianity we did a century ago, its fundamental principles continue to powerfully influence literature, academia, social issues, and political parties. Join Professor Birzer for a study in American history and politics, and how Catholics shaped our country in the past and will continue to do so in the future.

Course Lectures (30 min. per lecture)

1. Settling North America
2. The Colonies
3. Charles Carroll
4. The Second Great Awakening
5. Alexis de Tocqueville's America
6. Progressivism, Nationalism, and the "Greater Good
7. The Moral Imagination
8. The 20th Century

Course No. C60101 • Available Formats include: 4 DVD Set, 4 Audio CD Set, Video Download, Audio Download, Group Study Edition

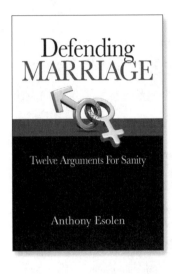

Powerful ammunition against cultural insanity

Anthony Esolen, Ph.D.

In this compelling defense of traditional marriage, Anthony Esolen uses moral, theological, and cultural arguments to defend this holy institution. Learn why gay marriage is a metaphysical impossibility, how legal sanction of gay marriage threatens the family, how the state becomes a religion when it attempts to elevate gay marriage, how divorce and sexual license have brought marriage to the brink, and how today's culture has emptied love of its true meaning.

978-1-61890-604-5 • Paperbound

What happened to liberty and justice for all?

James Tonkowich

Americans are losing constitutionally promised rights at an alarming pace. Both a chilling wake-up call and a clear call to action to Christians everywhere, *The Liberty Threat* illustrates how the rigid separation of Church and state has created a world is hostile to true faith. While the Founding Fathers understood the essentiality of religious practice unimpeded by government, time and cultural change has eroded this from the consciences of modern politicians.

978-1-61890-641-0 • Paperbound

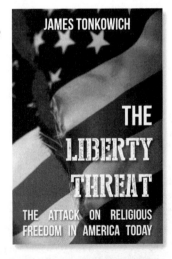

Best-Selling Bibles From SAINT BENEDICT+PRESS

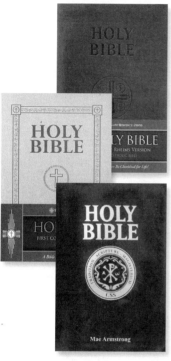

Douay Rheims Edition

One of the most trusted English translations of the Latin Vulgate, originally published in English 1600's and revised by Bishop Challoner. Our Douay Rheims Bible is offered in classic, high-quality covers, with gold-edges and a ribbon marker.

978-1935302-03-2 • Genuine Leather Black
978-1935302-05-6 • Paperbound
978-1935302-02-5 • Premium UltraSoft Burgundy

Gold-embossed Sacramental Bible

Contains colorful images, child-friendly Saints stories, daily Catholic prayers, and explanations of the Seven Sacraments and the Mass.

978-193530-241-4 • Hardcover White

Catholic Scripture Study International Bible

Integrates Sacred Scripture with extensive study materials and reference guides. Includes 76 full color inserts, Biblical Apologetics, Topical Index with over 130 Topics and 1100 Biblical References. Complete list of Biblical Abbreviations.

978-1935302-49-0 • Bonded Leather Black

Revised Standard Version – Catholic Edition

Translated from original languages during the 1940-1950's, this contemporary version is widely used by orthodox scholars.

978-1935302-06-3 • Genuine Leather Black
978-1935302-10-0 • Paperbound
978-1935302-09-4 • Premium UltraSoft Burgundy
978-193530-227-8 • Premium UltraSoft Black Large Print

TAN · CLASSICS

A collection of the finest literature in the Catholic tradition.

978-0-89555-227-3

978-0-89555-154-2

978-0-89555-155-9

Our TAN Classics collection is a well-balanced sampling of the finest literature in the Catholic tradition.

978-0-89555-230-3

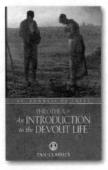

978-0-89555-228-0

978-0-89555-151-1

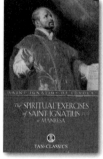

978-0-89555-153-5

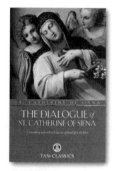

978-0-89555-149-8

978-0-89555-199-3

The collection includes distinguished spiritual works of the saints, philosophical treatises and famous biographies.

978-0-89555-226-6

978-0-89555-152-8

978-0-89555-225-9

 SAINT BENEDICT✝PRESS

Saint Benedict Press publishes books, Bibles, and multimedia
that explore and defend the Catholic intellectual tradition.
Our mission is to present the truths of the Catholic faith in
an attractive and accessible manner.

Founded in 2006, our name pays homage to the guiding
influence of the Rule of Saint Benedict and the Benedictine
monks of Belmont Abbey, just a short distance from our
headquarters in Charlotte, NC.

Saint Benedict Press publishes under several imprints. Our
TAN Books imprint (TANBooks.com), publishes over 500
titles in theology, spirituality, devotions, Church doctrine,
history, and the Lives of the Saints. Our Catholic Courses
imprint (CatholicCourses.com) publishes audio and video
lectures from the world's best professors in Theology,
Philosophy, Scripture, Literature and more.

For a free catalog, visit us online at
TANBooks.com

Or call us toll-free at
(800) 437-5876